Bottlekatz
A Complete Care Guide
for Orphan Kittens

Sharon Darrow

First Edition 2003

Second Edition 2013

ISBN 978-1-4116-6653-5

Publisher: Sharon S Darrow
Distributor Lulu.com

ACKNOWLEDGMENTS

Everything I am sharing in this book came directly from working with kittens. It is hard work that will often break your heart; however, these helpless little guys give so incredibly much in return.

Caring for kittens involves everyone in a household. My husband, Stan, has been amazingly patient and supportive throughout the years. My daughters, Shelley Young and Sheryl Wilson, and my grandchildren, Stan Young, Nicole Young Tilton, Christopher and Nicholas Wilson, have all been wonderful and made a huge difference with our kittens.

Working in rescue for years can take a huge toll, and I couldn't have done it without my incredible best friend, Ann Dickson. We all need someone to share the triumphs and painful losses, and she has always been there for me.

Throughout this book I remind you repeatedly to work with a good vet. Dr. Rene Case has always been a fountain of knowledge, and a good friend. Another amazing vet, Dr. Sandra McRoberts, deserves enormous gratitude and appreciation for her time and dedication to the cats and kittens in the Sacramento and Roseville area.

Most people doing rescue have resident pets in their home, and sometimes forget the sacrifices those animals must make when we are involved with rescue. In addition, the nurturing and lessons they provide are a vital part in raising healthy, well-adjusted kittens. I am grateful to my pets, and remind you to remember and appreciate yours as well.

Throughout this book I address readers as foster parents since my focus is on rescue, but the advice is exactly the same if you are someone raising a kitten or two for your own. I hope my experiences will be of value to you all.

Table of Contents

Chapter One

Introduction

SHOULD YOU FOSTER BOTTLE BABIES?

All those kittens are so adorable and you would really love to help --
but is fostering babies the best way for you to assist in rescue?
Please take the time to carefully consider everything <u>before</u> you take
some into your home. It is much better to say no initially than to
either do a poor job of mothering or decide to pass the babies on to
somebody else after taking them in. It is a big commitment and not
one to make on a whim.

HOW MANY ARE THERE?

This is always the first question people ask when they are
approached about taking kittens, even though it should come after
the age determination. The number is important in calculating the
amount of time and intensive care the kittens will require. Again, you
should be brutally honest with yourself about the amount of time and
emotional energy you can realistically give to the babies.

If you have no kittens already, taking in a litter of six or seven is a big
job, but should not be a problem for anyone willing to foster. If you
already have several babies, you need to look at their age
compatibility and whether adding new ones is practical. If you
cannot take the whole litter, **please DO NOT** separate them.
Littermates need each other and should always stay together, just
like children from the same family. It is much kinder to just say no
and try to help find someone who can take them all.

The old song about one being the loneliest number is very true for
kittens! Taking in a single kitten is great while they are tiny -- they
stay clean and are easy to care for. When they get about two weeks
old you should start looking around for some companions for them.

Company gives them comfort (a snuggle partner), someone to play with, and a source of valuable lessons when they get older and start learning to use their teeth and claws to play.

HOW OLD ARE THEY?

This is the most important question to ask, since the care required by the different ages is dramatically different. Kittens vary greatly in size and development, so it is always best to make your own determination of age, rather than relying on someone else's estimate Here are the key things to look for:

The umbilical cord is still present

The umbilical cord normally falls off at three to five days of age. If the kittens still have their cords, they are generally less than five days old.

The eyes are still closed

The eyes normally open at eight to ten days of age. So if the eyes are not yet opened, assume the kittens are less than ten days old.

On rare occasions the eyes do not open on time by themselves. If the age indicators in this chapter seem to indicate a kitten older than ten days, such as teeth coming through and walking upright with their bellies off the ground, the eyes need attention. Use a wet piece of gauze or cloth and rub the eyes, since they might be stuck closed. If that works for even a tiny spot, wait one day for them to finish opening. Don't be surprised if some unpleasant smelling white liquid pops out, just clean it off thoroughly.
Eyes need to open at the proper time, so if the kittens eyes don't open by themselves or with your gentle assistance for a kitten twelve days or older, you need the help of a vet or experienced mentor to get the eyes open immediately. The kitten will not act sick, but you must not ignore this in the hope that the eyes will fix themselves. Ignoring eyes that do not open at the time can cause blindness.

The umbilical cords are gone and the eyes are open

Now it gets tougher! The primary way to determine age for kittens that have their eyes open is twofold, the way they move and their teeth.

Kittens start out walking right away, but the youngest ones kind of drag their bellies because their legs are so shaky. As they get older, the leg strength increases and the balance improves, so movement is a very important factor. Babies up to about 2 to 2-1/2 weeks walk very carefully but still wobble a bit. Steady legs and pretty good balance generally says they are from 2-1/2 to 3-1/2 or 4 weeks old. The next step is running, which they generally start from 3-1/2 to 4 weeks old.

Just like kids, kittens develop as little individuals, so you need to check the teeth along with observing their movement. Those teeth are needle-sharp when they come in, but you need to check with your finger because just looking is really not enough. The first teeth to come through the gums are the tiny ones in the very front of the mouth, and they appear at about two weeks. After that the side teeth will push through. If you check the mouth and find front teeth, but nothing on the sides, you know they are not more than two weeks. At about 2-1/2 weeks you will feel very swollen gums on the sides of the mouth, with perhaps a point or two through. The side teeth should be all through the gums by 3-1/2 weeks, but not really fully erupted till the four-week stage. Pretty handy, since that is the stage they are ready to begin the weaning process.

Sometimes you might peg a kitten's age by their interest in eating solid foods. This can be misleading, since they might be extremely hungry and just trying to nurse at anything that smells edible. Be sure to check the other indicators for age first, and then make the proper care decisions, so that you do not stress out an immature tummy.

After you get the answers to these vital questions, it is time to prepare for your new babies. For ease in looking up information, we are dividing nursing kittens into four different age groups:

GROUP #1   Birth to ten days

GROUP #2   Eleven days to 2-1/2 weeks

GROUP #3   2-1/2 weeks for four weeks

GROUP #4   Four weeks and older

Two-hours old is not very big

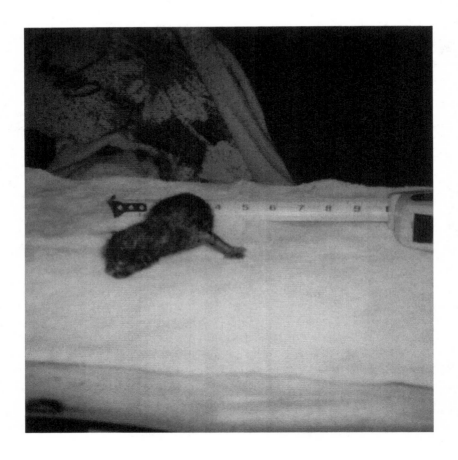

Top-opening carrier with litter of kittens

Chapter Two

What Do You Need?

Congratulations! You have apparently decided to become a kitty parent. Now you need to assemble all the supplies and materials that your new babies will need. Once again, even though the basics are the same, the specific needs will differ based on the age of the kittens. For a comprehensive breakdown and comparison, take a look at the charts at the end of the chapter.

Carrier/Container

Everyone who does rescue of any kind needs to have a good carrier on hand. Even if you do not use it as a home for the orphan kittens, you will need it for trips to the vet office, to your kitty mentor for assistance, and eventually to the site where the babies can be shown for adoption. Boxes of the appropriate size can make perfectly fine homes for babies, but they are NOT an acceptable alternative for transporting the animals.

The size of the container (home) depends on the age and number of the kittens. Group one (1-10 days) babies do not move much and just need enough room for their heat source, bedding, and a little crawling room. Group two (11 days to 2-1/2 weeks) babies have their eyes open and need to start exercising their legs. They need more space to start walking around. Group three (2-1/2 weeks to 4 weeks) babies are making some real changes. During this period they are starting to look for a place away from their beds to go potty (but still will soak and mess their bedding) and even to begin the weaning process. A box or carrier is fine for their beds, but they need additional room to walk around in, as well as for a beginning litter box and dishes for food and water. It is very important that they are not confined in their bed areas because you do not want them to get used to going potty on bedding. Group four (4 weeks and older) babies definitely need room. They need all the same things as Group three, as well as for running and playing.

Bedding

Any absorbent material is fine for bedding, as long as it can be washed and bleached in very hot water and then thrown in the dryer. Old toweling or blanket materials work well, but is is very important that any dangling strings are cut off and that there no holes. Babies can get caught and tangled -- even strangled -- in holes or by strings. Group one and two babies particularly like material with a nap (fake fur, lambswool, etc.) to cuddle into. Those youngest babies also like stuffed toys in their beds to cuddle up with, but the toys should be washed, bleached, and machine dried frequently for sanitary reasons.

Heat Source

A good heat source is essential for Group 1 and Group 2 babies regardless of the weather or room temperature. The heat source not only helps keep them warm, but also provides comfort similar to their momma cat's warm body. Group 3 and 4 still appreciate having the heat source in their bedding area.

There are several different kinds of heat source items you can use, all with their advantages and drawbacks. The one item that we recommend you NOT use is an electric heating pad. Not only are these inconvenient because you are tied to the proximity of an outlet, but heating pads are just a tragic accident waiting to happen. Heating pads can fail and overheat the babies, while the size and shape of the pads make them difficult for the kittens to escape if they are too hot. Heating pads are not designed to run continuously for extended periods, but kittens need a constant heat source for weeks.

An old-fashioned hot water bottle can be a great source. They hold their heat for a long time, are relatively inexpensive, and are easy to keep clean. They should aways be placed inside a sealed heavy-duty plastic bag, like a zip-lock freezer bag, then wrapped in a towel and placed in the carrier so that the kittens can get away from them if they are too hot. The drawbacks are that they can be hard to find, and you have to be extremely careful about leakage. Always place the water bottle with the neck pointed up for safety. Old water bottles can spring leaks along the seams, so be sure to carefully check before placing them in with the kittens. These precautions are necessary even when the hot water bottle is sealed in the plastic bag, because sometimes the plastic bags can have faulty seams or pinholes in them, so you cannot be complacent about the potential for leaks.

A very simple, effective and inexpensive heat source is a rice pack. Just fill an old tube sock, preferably a man's calf-high sock, about 2/3 full with uncooked white rice, tie off the top, and heat in the microwave for a couple of minutes. The sock will hold heat for a couple of hours, is it is very soft and comfy for the babies to curl up to. The sock should look and feel firm, kind of like a cloth sausage, when it's tied off. It's a good idea to cover the rice pack with a towel or blanket to keep the baby from getting too hot, and to help conserve the heat. When the rice pack gets cold, just heat it up again. When it gets dirty from urine and feces (and it will), untie it, discard the rice, and wash the sock. It is a good idea to make several, so you can put them on both sides of the cage or carrier for better heating, but always leave some open space for the kittens to crawl away if they are uncomfortable. If you don't have white rice on hand, you can use small beans or lentils as a substitute.

There are also new items coming out all the time that are designed to provide low, safe heat for animals. Just make sure that they are safe, made by a reputable company, and that the cost merits the investment. Remember that it is vitally important that they can be easily cleaned and disinfected. A heat source appropriate for an adult cat or dog may not be safe for tiny kittens.

Group #1 Carrier, view #1

Group #1 Carrier, view #2

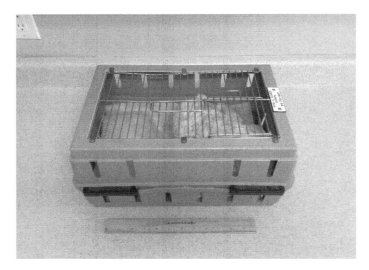

Group #2 Carrier, View #1

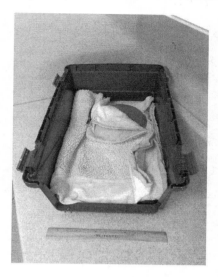

Group #2 Carrier, View #2

Group #3 Cage

Group #4 Cage

Formula

Many rescue people like to use home made formulas or goat's milk for feeding kittens while others prefer commercial kitten formulas. I personally think that goat's milk is a perfect food -- for baby goats. Even though a lot of people swear by it and by home made formulas, I have two concerns: first of all, are you sure that the goat's milk or formula has all the nutrients that the kittens need for proper growth? And secondly, are you sure that each and every batch you make is exactly the same? Kittens, like many human babies, have very sensitive tummies that get upset when the food is varied. The resulting vomiting and diarrhea can be very debilitating for them and for the foster parent.

Commercial formulas make it easier to check the nutritive value, but again, you want to be sure that you have a consistent source of supply. Some brands are only available through vet offices, while others are not always on the pet store shelves. If you are not extremely careful about planning ahead, you can get into a situation where you have to substitute a different brand with the same potential gastric upset problems outlined above.

Consistency is important even with the same brand of formula. KMR has been my favorite for over 20 years and has been easy to find. KMR (Kitten Milk Replacer) comes in both liquid and powdered forms. You need to decide which type you are going to use since switching back and forth can create the same type of tummy problems that you would see from switching back and forth between different brands. Base your choice on availability and convenience for you, and then stick with it. Of course, if you have a kitten that has gastric problems or is not thriving, changing the formula is something worth trying.

It is extremely important that you take note of the expiration times for the formula you choose. KMR liquid must be discarded 72 hours after the can is opened, and is so expensive that you don't want to waste any of it. If you use liquid KMR, keep what you will use in a couple of days in a closed container in the refrigerator. Do not store the formula in the refrigerator in the original can because you can't shake it easily without spilling. The best containers I've found are small, thoroughly cleaned plastic water or soda bottles. They can be shaken safely to mix the formula. The water or soda bottles are also very easy to use for filling the baby bottles without spillage. The formula that won't be used during the initial 72 hours (for KMR, the time may be different for other types of formula) can be frozen in small portions (sandwich bags work fine) until you need them. The frozen formula turns dark, but will thaw and change colors when you are ready for it.

Check your formula and make sure that you are using and storing it properly. You should also check your formula to see if it has colostrum in it, since that is only appropriate for the youngest kittens.

Bottles & Nipples

There are a wide variety of types and brands of bottles available, and it really doesn't make a lot of difference what you choose. It is important that they are easy to fill, handle, and thoroughly clean. There are two sizes that are common, a small one that holds about four tablespoons and a larger one that holds four ounces. The small one is best for very young kittens or a small number of them because you don't want the formula to spoil. The larger bottles are wonderful for older babies or large litters so you don't have to keep filling bottles.

The type of nipples you choose can make an enormous difference. Many kittens will refuse to suckle or will fight the bottle just because they don't like the nipple. Unfortunately, the most common type of nipple available is the worst one. The nipples that come prepackaged with most bottles in pet stores look like miniature human baby nipples, but frustrate kittens and should be thrown away immediately -- but be sure to keep the bottle and nipple ring. The best nipple available is made by Four Paws. It is available in some pet stores or feed stores and can be special ordered. They are also available online -- my favorite source is a supplier for squirrel rescue. Pet stores may be able to get them for you packaged in boxes of four, and the squirrel rescue source online has them in bags of 100. The nipples are inexpensive, and should be stockpiled by any rescue group or active foster home. These nipples fit on any standard bottles with the bottle rings that came that came packaged with the bottle. All you have to do is throw away the nipple and substitute the one from Four Paws.

Some pet stores also carry nipples with very long, very narrow nipples. These are sometimes helpful with newborns or premies, but not generally liked by older kittens.

You usually want to read and follow the manufacturer's directions for their products; however, you should just ignore the nipple directions. Forget the heated needle or razor and use a sharp pair of scissors. Just cut off the very tip of the nipple. There will be a good-sized hole; however, the kittens suckling will form a tight seal that allows the flow rate that the baby needs. You should not have to worry about the kitten choking or aspirating formula as long as you hold the baby in a position that mimics that of a normal nursing kitten -- NEVER put a kitten on its back to nurse.

Common Types of Kitten Bottle Nipples

The top left nipple is the most common you will find in pet stores, but kittens generally do not like it. If you can find a different type, throw this one away.

The bottom left nipple is sometimes good for very, very tiny kittens, but not generally liked by older ones.

The best nipples available are by Four Paws, and come packaged four to a box or 100 in a bag, as show here. The top right nippled is right out of the box, while the lower right nipple has had the tip cut for use.

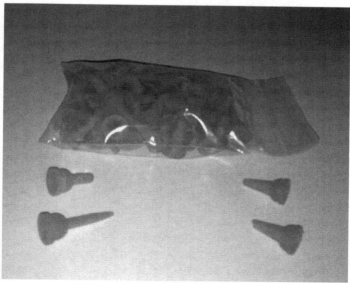

Cotton Balls

Cotton balls or cosmetic puffs work great for stimulating the kitten to urinate and defecate, and for cleaning the genital area. They are soft, inexpensive, and help keep your fingers dry and clean. You can buy the jumbo size at most grocery stores or drugs stores and then put them in a large, sealed plastic kitchen storage bag for easy use.

I have used paper towels, toilet paper, rags, etc. for stimulating and cleaning, but found that the cotton balls seem to be the easiest for me to use, and the easiest on the kittens' skin. If you prefer to use some other type of material, just be sure that it is soft and absorbent. If you decide to use some type of cloth, be sure to wash and bleach it frequently.

Babywipes

Very young kittens are messy! Even though you routinely stimulate them to urinate and defecate, they still get covered with everything imaginable. Bathing constantly is not practical, so babywipes can be a great alternative. Generic brands from discount stores can be an excellent choice for price and convenience, as long as they have no alcohol, perfume or dye.

Karo Syrup

If you are lucky, you will never need to use this for your kittens. Karo syrup, or any white corn syrup for cooking, is the cure for a life-threatening condition called hypoglycemic shock (low blood sugar). Since a low blood sugar level happens with no notice and requires fast treatment, it is always best to have karo syrup on hand. Check your expiration date, since this is an item found in most kitchens, but used infrequently.

Scales

Weighing kittens daily is one of the easiest, most foolproof ways to measure their health. You need a scale that will measure in increments as small as 1/4 to 1/2 ounce. Postal or food scales work great, since they generally go up to at least five pounds and can be calibrated to zero with a dish or box secured in place for holding the kitten. Traditional baby or pet scales usually measure in increments of two ounces, so are not fine enough for kittens.

Antibiotic

A broad-spectrum antibiotic, which has to be prescribed by a vet, should be on hand. I used clavamox for years, but there are other choices available now as well. My statistics show that automatically giving an antibiotic to kittens does a good job of helping to counteract the loss of immunity from their mother's milk. I always gave clavamox to any kittens I took in that were two weeks or younger when they arrived.

Clavamox, and most other antibiotics you might use, comes in powder form and needs to be hydrated. Check with your mentor or vet to make sure you have know the proper amount of water to add, so you can keep the powder on hand and mix it up when needed. Do NOT adjust the water levels for any reason. You must mix it properly for the antibiotic to work. Once mixed, most antibiotics need to be kept in the refrigerator, so be sure to follow the mentor or vet's instructions. The dosage amount will depend on the kitten's weight. For clavamox, the rule of thumb is .1- mil per pound (look close, that is POINT 10 mil, otherwise known as one tenth of one mil), using .10 as a minimum dose. That means you give .10 mil to the smallest newborn up to anything weighing about one pound, then go up accordingly. You give the clavamox twice daily for 10 days. Remember, just like with humans, finish out the treatment even if the kittens look like they don't need it. If you are using a different antibiotic, be sure to use the proper dosage and treatment program.

You will need to work with an experienced foster or vet in order to get the clavamox, or other broad-spectrum antibiotic, since treating kittens in this manner is NOT sanctioned by the drug companies or vets as a normal protocol. A vet that has not worked in rescue will tell you that using an antibiotic in this manner may cause the kitten to be extra sensitive to antibiotics later in life, and they are absolutely correct. Since the survival rate of kittens less than a week old is extremely low (an they are not out of the woods until they reach four weeks old), I have found that the improvement in survival rate is an acceptable tradeoff.

Syringes

You never know when you might need to administer karo syrup, force-feed, or give medication to your kittens. For this reason it is a good idea to have some syringes on hand. For most uses a I mil syringe is the best, although it is helpful to also have a 3 mil syringe on hand as well.

Thermometer

Like the karo syrup and syringes, this is an item you should have on hand in case of emergencies. You should have a separate thermometer for your kittens, well marked for your family's hygiene. A good digital thermometer is much better than an old-fashioned mercury type. Also, be sure that you have lubricant with the thermometer for those tiny bottoms, even though you will only insert the tip. KY jelly, petroleum jelly or mineral oil are all fine. A normal temperature reading for cats and kittens is from 101 to 102 degrees.

Litter

If you want to start a heated discussion among rescue people, just open a conversation about which is the best litter. There are pros and cons for just about everything available, so you should use what you personally prefer, especially if you have resident cats in the house. Here are a few things to consider about some of the most common types:

Clay

This is the favorite, which people like because it is cheap and readily available. It is also heavy, the pieces often have sharp edges for tender paws, and it forms a smelly urine layer at the bottom of the pan. If you choose this type, you must be sure to clean the pan thoroughly and frequently, then refilling with fresh litter each time.

Scoopable

This is easy to find, reasonable in cost, and good at odor control. It also sticks to tender wet skin and fur and gets stuck between baby toes. If you use this kind, be sure to keep the box very clean and to carefully check the kittens' bodies and remove any litter that might have stuck to the fur.

Some people claim that kittens eat this litter and can die. While it is physically possible, I have yet to find a documented case through the internet or vets that I've met. Very young kittens will taste whatever litter you provide, which is why it is critical that they are watched carefully as they get used to the litter box regardless of the type of litter you use.

Silica Crystals

This is lightweight, great at odor control, and easy to use. It is also sometimes sharp on baby feet and the jagged pieces can get lodged inside the kitten's mouth. The type that comes in jagged pieces really hurts when you step on pieces that are on the floor -- especially when you are barefoot and sleepy for that late night feeding. And the type that comes in round pieces can end up making a big mess when the little balls roll all over the floor when kicked or spread out of the box.

Ground Corn Litter

This is lightweight and can be inexpensive if you buy a generic brand. It is not very good at odor control, so you must be sure to clean it often. One serious drawback is that you must NOT use a corn-based dry kitten food for kittens using this type of litter because the kittens will sometimes eat the litter when they smell the similarity to their food. I have personally seen most of a litter die in this manner, and the foster family was devastated.

See what I mean? I have tried various different litters and combinations throughout the years, and am back to using scoopable for all the kittens. Whatever you use requires close observation, a high degree of safety awareness, and constant cleaning. One big no-no -- do not train kittens on either paper or cloth. If you do, they will learn the lesson too well and then later in life will not understand the problem when they potty on your newspaper or magazine, or in the pile of laundry on the floor. Good litter training is extremely important for success later in life. Poor litter training is almost always a cause for an adopted cat to either be returned, tossed outside, or taken to the pound.

Weaning Food

Do not waste your money buying special commercial weaning food, no matter who makes it. Most kittens do not like it (I have never seen a single one that ate it willingly), so you are just creating frustration for everyone. The best weaning food is a mixture of a small amount of canned cat food for taste and aroma, and water softened kitten dry food.

Dishes

Regular cat food and water dishes are not always the best things for kittens. Kittens are going to walk in the dishes, and on the rims. You need to avoid dishes that tip easily or are too deep to reach inside. Very heavy, flat dishes or pans work well, as do paper or plastic plates. Old-fashioned, nearly flat glass ashtrays (check at thrift shops or garage sales) work great for the tiniest kittens.

Toys

Healthy kittens love to play, and watching them is one of the great joys of fostering. You need to be very careful about safety, however. I also like to make sure that toys can be washed and disinfected, so they are safe from one group to another. Fuzzy mice, soft balls, all types of toys to bat about on the floor, or interactive wand toys are always popular, as are old household items like paper bags (NOT plastic), wadded up paper balls, the plastic twist tops on milk bottles, hair "scrunchies" and cable ties. Do NOT let them play with string, twine or ribbon, no matter how cute it is to watch. When anything like string gets in the mouth it is easier to swallow than spit out, and then the baby keeps swallowing more as they try to get away. This spells tragedy when the stuff gets entangled in the intestines, requiring either expensive and dangerous surgery or putting the kitten down. Another toy to avoid is the small, hard plastic ball with cutouts in the side, sometimes with bells or other items inside. The kittens can get their teeth caught in the holes and then panic. This is a very, very dangerous potential that is easily prevented by just avoiding those types of toy balls.

Scratching Posts

Early training makes a great difference to future success. Put out lots of acceptable items for scratching, like posts, condos or climbing trees. Try different textures too, like rope or corrugated cardboard. There are lots of very inexpensive types available, so try different ones. Remember that these items must be fairly easy to clean and disinfect, or cheap enough to replace often.

This is one of those items that is far more important than one might think. Scratching furniture or household items is another very common reasons for an adopted cat to be returned to the foster, thrown out of the house, or taken to the pound. Early diligence can make the difference between a successful adoption and a potential tragedy.

Shampoo

When you bathe kittens it is important to remember three key things: the shampoo must be gentle to eyes, skin and coat, and not contain any chemicals that might be irritating or dangerous. There are good kitten/puppy shampoos available, but I recommend old-fashioned baby shampoo. As long as you are not bathing more frequently than every few days it will not dry the coat or skin. If you use commercially prepared kitten shampoo, make sure that it does NOT contain any extra chemicals for flea or parasite control.

Many people have watched programs on television showing Dawn dish soap being used to remove oil and then assumed it was fine for kittens. Do not use dish soap of any kind. It is much too strong for kitten skin and coats, and will burn their eyes.

Hair Dryer

After bathing it is critical that the kitten be thoroughly dried. You can purchase professional cage dryers, but they are bulky and expensive. They also need the animal to be in a cage in the open. I prefer to use a regular human blow dryer and my hands to dry and fluff the kitten very quickly. You want the temperature to be warm to dry the fur quickly, but if the air is too hot for your hands as they fluff the kitten's fur, it is too hot for the kitten.

Veterinarian

Every rescue person needs to develop a relationship with a good vet. Take time to choose someone you trust and like. The best vet for a rescue relationship is one that works with rescue groups, since he or she will generally offer special reduced pricing and understands the unique problems and challenges that rescue animals bring. If your personal vet does not meet these criteria, check with local rescue groups for a recommendation.

Mentor

This can absolutely make the difference between success and failure, frustration and confidence. Your vet is there for medical concerns, but the mentor can be available for the questions that come up about routine care and behavior. They also can help you make the decision on when a visit to the vet is necessary. A good mentor should be fairly easy to reach whenever you need them -- but remember, they are probably very busy with kitten calls in addition to their regular life demands and might have to call you back. Again, don't be afraid to contact local rescue groups, vets, or even pet shops when you need a referral for someone to help you.

EASY REFERENCE SUPPLY CHARTS BY AGE GROUPS:

ITEM	FIRST AGE GROUP 0 - 10 DAYS
Carrier/Container	Small carrier is fine. Needs easy access and just enough room for heat source and babies
Bedding	Any towels or material that can be washed, bleached, and put in the dryer. They especially enjoy fake fur material to snuggle into.
Heat Source	Rice packs, heat disks, hot water bottles, etc. NOT ELECTRIC HEATING PADS.
Food	Commercial kitten formula -- recommend KMR
Bottles & Nipples	Any pet sized bottle, with nipple ring. Recommend the "Four Paws" nipple, with just the tip cut off by sharp scissors.
Cotton balls	Cotton balls or synthetic puffs for stimulation and gentle cleaning.
Babywipes	Use for cleaning, but NOT for cleaning eyes.
Karo Syrup	Keep on hand for use in case of hypoglycemic shock
Scales	Any kind of scales is fine, as long as it will register partial ounces. Scales that show increments of 2 ounces is NOT fine enough.
Antibiotic	Use for all new orphans to provide immunity source

Syringes	1 mil size for antibiotics or karo. 3 mil and 5 mil are good to have on hand as well
Thermometer	Keep a digital on hand, with lubricant
Litterbox	Not needed
Litter	Not needed
Weaning Food	Not needed
Dishes	Not needed
Toys	Babies love a stuffed animal to cuddle -- but it MUST be washable, bleachable, and dryable
Scratching posts	Not needed
Nail Trimmers	Small cat nail trimmers or human fingernail clippers will work fine
Shampoo	Kitten shampoo (NO PESTICIDES OR CHEMICALS), or baby shampoo
Hair Dryer	Any hand-held blow dryer on medium setting
Mentor	Find someone who is patient, compassionate, and has lots of orphan kitten experience. They should be available by phone whenever there is a problem that warrants a personal look.
Veterinarian	Find one who is patient, compassionate, and has lots of orphan kitten experience.

ITEM	SECOND AGE GROUP 11 DAYS TO 2-1/2 WEEKS
Carrier/Container	Small carrier is fine. Needs easy access and room for the babies to walk around and explore.
Bedding	Any towels or material that can be washed, bleached, and put in the dryer. They especially enjoy fake fur material to snuggle into.
Heat Source	Rice packs, heat disks, hot water bottles, etc. NOT ELECTRIC HEATING PADS.
Food	Commercial kitten formula -- recommend KMR
Bottles & Nipples	Any pet sized bottle, with nipple ring. Recommend the "Four Paws" nipple, with just the tip cut off by sharp scissors.
Cotton balls	Cotton balls or synthetic puffs for stimulation and gentle cleaning.
Babywipes	Use for cleaning, but NOT for cleaning eyes.
Karo Syrup	Keep on hand for use in case of hypoglycemic shock
Scales	Any kind of scales is fine, as long as it will register partial ounces. Scales that show increments of 2 ounces is NOT fine enough.
Antibiotic	Use for all new orphans to provide immunity source

Syringes	1 mil size for antibiotics or karo. 3 mil and 5 mil are good to have on hand as well
Thermometer	Keep a digital on hand, with lubricant
Litterbox	Not needed
Litter	Not needed
Weaning Food	Not needed
Dishes	Not needed
Toys	Babies love a stuffed animal to cuddle -- but it MUST be washable, bleachable, and dryable
Scratching posts	Not needed
Nail Trimmers	Small cat nail trimmers or human fingernail clippers will work fine
Shampoo	Kitten shampoo (NO PESTICIDES OR CHEMICALS), or baby shampoo
Hair Dryer	Any hand-held blow dryer on medium setting
Mentor	Find someone who is patient, compassionate, and has lots of orphan kitten experience. They should be available by phone whenever there is a problem that warrants a personal look.
Veterinarian	Find one who is patient, compassionate, and has lots of orphan kitten experience.

ITEM	THIRD AGE GROUP 2-1/2 WEEKS to 4 WEEKS
Carrier/Container	Carrier is fine for the bed area, but they need a box or cage around it so they have room for a litterbox, water, food dish, and room to exercise and explore
Bedding	Any towels or material that can be washed, bleached, and put in the dryer. They especially enjoy fake fur material to snuggle into.
Heat Source	Rice packs, heat disks, hot water bottles, etc. NOT ELECTRIC HEATING PADS.
Food	Commercial kitten formula -- recommend KMR. In addition, you will need softened dry kitten food and canned food to start the weaning process
Bottles & Nipples	Any pet sized bottle, with nipple ring. Recommend the "Four Paws" nipple, with just the tip cut off by sharp scissors.
Cotton balls	Cotton balls or synthetic puffs for stimulation and gentle cleaning.
Babywipes	Use for cleaning, but NOT for cleaning eyes.
Karo Syrup	Keep on hand for use in case of hypoglycemic shock
Scales	Any kind of scales is fine, as long as it will register partial ounces. Scales that show increments of 2 ounces is NOT fine enough.

Antibiotic	Use for all new orphans to provide immunity source
Syringes	1 mil size for antibiotics or karo. 3 mil and 5 mil are good to have on hand as well
Thermometer	Keep a digital on hand, with lubricant
Litterbox	Use very shallow, disposable pans with shallow layer of litter
Litter	Use something you like, but clean constantly and watch closely. All litters have dangers and drawbacks that require vigilance.
Weaning Food	Not really needed for most kittens till about 3-1/2 weeks. Use a wet mix of dry kitten food with canned for taste and smell appeal
Dishes	Dishes should be shallow and non-tippable. They will be walked in regularly, so must be cleaned constantly.
Toys	Some simple balls and fuzzy mice toys might start getting attention at this age.
Scratching posts	Not needed
Nail Trimmers	Small cat nail trimmers or human fingernail clippers will work fine
Shampoo	Kitten shampoo (NO PESTICIDES OR CHEMICALS), or baby shampoo
Hair Dryer	Any hand-held blow dryer on medium setting

Mentor	Find someone who is patient, compassionate, and has lots of orphan kitten experience. They should be available by phone whenever there is a problem that warrants a personal look.
Veterinarian	Find one who is patient, compassionate, and has lots of orphan kitten experience.

ITEM	FOURTH AGE GROUP 4 WEEKS AND OLDER
Carrier/Container	Carrier is fine for the bed area, but they need room for their water, litterbox, food, and toys. They also need to be able to start running and playing to exercise and strengthen their muscles.
Bedding	Any towels or material that can be washed, bleached, and put in the dryer. They especially enjoy fake fur material to snuggle into.
Heat Source	Rice packs, heat disks, hot water bottles, etc. NOT ELECTRIC HEATING PADS.
Food	Commercial kitten formula -- recommend KMR for "comfort" bottles. Dry food available all the time, wet mix of canned and dry food periodically during the day.
Bottles & Nipples	Any pet sized bottle, with nipple ring. Recommend the "Four Paws" nipple, with just the tip cut off by sharp scissors.
Cotton balls	Should no longer be needed for stimulation.
Babywipes	Use for cleaning, but NOT for cleaning eyes.
Karo Syrup	Keep on hand for use in case of hypoglycemic shock
Scales	Any kind of scales is fine, as long as it will register partial ounces. Scales that show increments of 2 ounces is NOT fine enough.

Antibiotic	Use for all new orphans to provide immunity source
Syringes	1 mil size for antibiotics or karo. 3 mil and 5 mil are good to have on hand as well
Thermometer	Keep a digital on hand, with lubricant
Litterbox	Use very shallow, disposable pans with shallow layer of litter
Litter	Use something you like, but clean constantly and watch closely. All litters have dangers and drawbacks that require vigilance.
Weaning Food	Use a wet mix of dry kitten food with canned
Dishes	Dishes should be shallow and non-tippable. They will be walked in regularly, so must be cleaned constantly.
Toys	Some simple balls and fuzzy mice type toys, as well as more complex "battable" things, and condos, paper bags or boxes to hide in.
Scratching posts	They will use simple scratching posts for climbing and playing.
Nail Trimmers	Small cat nail trimmers or human fingernail clippers will work fine
Shampoo	Kitten shampoo (NO PESTICIDES OR CHEMICALS), or baby shampoo
Hair Dryer	Any hand-held blow dryer on medium setting

Mentor	Find someone who is patient, compassionate, and has lots of orphan kitten experience. They should be available by phone whenever there is a problem that warrants a personal look.
Veterinarian	Find one who is patient, compassionate, and has lots of orphan kitten experience.

Some dogs are great baby-sitters!

Nobody will disturb this little guy's nap

Can't you just hear this kitten daring anybody to come get it -- and the poor dog begging mom to come rescue her

Chapter 3

Routine "How To's"

Wow! You are making progress. You have decided to be a kitty parent, made a decision on how old and how many to take in, and assembled most of the items you will need. Babies are on the way -- or already meowing at you -- and now you need to know exactly how to do everything. It is one thing to talk about bottle-feeding a kitten, and an entirely different thing to try to get this tiny, wiggling, squalling thing to actually nurse from the bottle.

Set up the bed and cage

The exact details of the beds will differ depending on the number and ages of the kittens; however, they all need to be comfy, warm, clean and safe.

Group one (0-10 days) kittens can easily be kept in a small carrier. The kind that opens on the top are especially nice, because they make it easy to see the kittens and to get them out for feeding and cleaning. Just be sure that the carrier has room for lots of clean bedding and the heat source, but is large enough that the kittens don't have to stay directly on the heat source if they are too warm. The carrier should be kept covered between feedings so the babies can sleep peacefully.

Group two (11 days to 2-1/2 weeks) kittens need a little more room. Moving up to a medium size carrier is an ideal change, because they need all the same kind of conditions as Group one, but with just a little more room to start using their legs.

Group three (2-1/2 weeks to 4 weeks) kittens should not be kept in a carrier because they need more mobility. A carrier makes a good bed area, but only if it is inside a larger cage. Cages need not be expensive, fancy animal enclosures -- in fact, most will not work because the little ones will walk right out between the bars. Big boxes from the grocery store (watermelon boxes for example) work well. U-Haul has a box (called the "flat wardrobe") that works great. The box should be something that you can easily access the kittens for feeding and cleaning, but also have adequate room for their bed, food and water dishes, a small flat litterbox, and a little open space for them to walk and play. A nice big box or cage will carry the kittens right through "Group four" requirements.

Group four (4 weeks and older) kittens have the same space needs as Group three, but need more room for playing. If you get a nice big box for them when they are "Group three," it should do fine as they grow, providing they get some free time each day to run and climb. This age works very well in a bathroom, or other small room -- just make sure it is "kitten proofed" for safety and good training. That means a non-carpeted floor so they cannot get used to pottying on the fabric. It also means no high objects that they might climb on and then fall off while playing. Beds in the room are a very bad idea, since they can use the bedding to help them climb up, but can then either get stranded and end up making messes on the bed or falling off and getting hurt. It is also a good idea to avoid furniture pieces that they can climb under because of the danger of them getting stuck and of them making messes in those dark corners.

Group one (0-10 days) kittens must be fed very frequently around the clock. If the kittens have their umbilical cords, start feeding every 1-1/2 to 2 hours, round the clock, then gradually lengthen the time by about 1/2 hour between feedings every few days. Remember that this is a very loose guideline, not something to hold to. It is vitally important to watch their weight so you know they are thriving on the feeding schedule. Do NOT feed them more often just because they are awake and crying, or you will run the risk of overfeeding them.

The best positions for feeding kittens is to closely mimic the way they would nurse from mom. They should be on their feet (or tummies) with the bottle just slightly tilted in front of them. Often they will put their front paws up against your hand and knead, just like they would against their mom. The kneading motion is natural, and helps bring down mom's milk, so they find it comforting. Remember that the position should be what is best for the kitten, rather than what is most convenient for you. Don't restrain or wrap them up, don't put them in positions where they are standing up against your body, and most important of all, do NOT ever feed them on their backs. Feeding a kitten on its back can permit the baby to aspirate milk into the lungs.

These kittens will not seek out the nipple by themselves, nor will they automatically know what to do with it. That means that you will need to get them started. If you hold your left hand over the kitten's head, you can then use your index finger to gently open the mouth from the side, then insert the nipple with the right hand. The nipple should be pressed very gently against the top of the baby's mouth to release just a drop or two of formula. Do NOT squeeze milk into the kitten's mouth because that can release too much at once. It normally takes just a short time for the kitten to get the idea and begin sucking. If they fall off, just repeat. If they are not interested, then try again later. Very young ones may only take just a tiny bit at each feeding, so don't try to force them.

Group two (11 days to 2-1/2 weeks) kittens are normally fed about every 4 to 5 hours. The frequency will slowly decrease as they grow older. Just be sure to watch their weight so you know they are thriving on the feeding schedule. Even though they are a little older, these kittens are not yet ready to go all night or all day without feedings, so be sure to arrange your schedule and alarm clock to keep their feedings regular around the clock.

The best positions for these to nurse is the same as the Group one kittens, but they are much more active when the nipple is in place. They may frantically wave their paws while you are trying to get it in their mouths, but just work with them. Don't restrain the paws or you will just frustrate them and make the whole process much more difficult. During this age group you will find that they will sometimes move the nipple to the side of their mouths and chew on it. No, they are not losing interest or trying to make life difficult. They are teething and chewing on the nipple feels good on their gums. Gently just move the nipple back to the front of their mouths if you can, but don't fight with them. As long as they are getting formula it doesn't matter if they are working from the side of the mouth; however, you can end up with a chewed off nipple. Good reason to make sure you have extra nipples available.

Group three (2-1/2 weeks to 4 weeks) kittens are normally fed about every 5 to 6 hours. The frequency will slowly decrease as they grow older. As you get toward the end of this age group you can start letting them sleep through the night, but pay close attention to their weight.

This age is a different kind of challenge, because if they are orphaned at this age they had lots of time to nurse from mom. That means that they are very aware of the difference between mom's warm nipple and this strange, cold rubber thing you are pushing in their mouth. When they get the idea of the formula they do fine, but it can take a little work. Do NOT fight with them or restrain them. They will get the idea if you are patient. Kittens in this group have lots of sharp teeth, so watch out for the nipple chewing and for indications that they are getting ready for weaning.

Group four (4 weeks and older) kittens are normally fed about every 6 to 8 hours, then just supplemental bottles through the weaning process. These guys do not need feeding during the night, but should always have food available to them between bottle feedings.

Taking in newly orphaned kittens of this age is hard because they would still be nursing from mom, but don't always take to the bottle. Sometimes this age can be started right in with the normal weaning routine if they are not interested in the bottle.

Sleeping, how often and how long?

Just a little note about kittens and sleeping arrangements. A lot of fosters think it's sweet and cute to have the babies sleep on their bodies or in their beds. This is NOT a good idea. Besides the obvious hygienic problems (moving around in their sleep will stimulate them to relieve their kidneys and bowels) and the possibility of them being smothered, sleeping with a human provides too much sensory input. The kittens will not sleep as deep and as long as they should. Also, like human babies, it is important that they learn to sleep by themselves or with their littermates. If they fall asleep on you sometimes, that is sweet and special, but it should not be the normal sleeping routine.

Group one (0 to 10 days) kittens do very little other than sleeping or eating. Like newborn babies, they will literally sleep all the time except when they are being fed. It is important that they have a quiet, comfortable, soft bed where they will not be disturbed, so covering the cage or carrier is important.

Group two (11 days to 2-1/2 weeks) kittens still do very little other than sleeping, but they will crawl and cry when they wake up. They recognize your voice, smell and touch, and will immediately start acting like they are starving when you open the carrier or touch them. Their sleep is very important though, so you should be careful not to wake them between feedings.

Group three (2-1/2 weeks to 4 weeks) kittens have added an important new activity -- play! It is so much fun to play with them and watch them, but you need to be careful to avoid overstimulation. Like little tiny kids, they will play like made and then practically drop in their tracks. As long as you pay attention and let them wake up when they are ready, they should get plenty of sleep.

Group four (4 weeks and older) kittens are very busy. They will play hard together or with you for yours, then plop down for a nap. Sleep is still extremely important, so you need to be sure that you don't push them too much. When they are sleeping or look like they want to go to sleep, don't distract or wake them until they are rested and ready.

Stimulating

Stimulating is the term we use to describe the process of helping the kittens go pee and poop. Okay, so it would be more proper to have said "urinate" and "defecate." This was deliberate though. If you are a little squeamish about the terms or the actual "stuff," you might want to rethink fostering. You will not only be paying a lot of attention to pee and poop, but cleaning it off everything constantly. And everything includes you. Just remember that everything will wash, and nobody has died yet from kitten pee or poop on his or her hands.

Stimulating kittens is a lot like cleaning babies. Not only is the process similar, so are the complaints. The way the kittens cry and squirm around you would think they were being killed, and the way their squirming can get stuff all over themselves and your hands, you might think they should be! Just do what needs to be done, and don't worry too much about the mess you're wearing until the job is done.

Group one (0 to 10 days) kittens need stimulating after each feeding. Use soft, absorbent material (I prefer the jumbo fake cotton balls) and stroke the lower tummy and genitals. Some people will tell you to wet the material first, but I suggest you start with dry. The material will be warm and wet right away and you will not have sacrificed absorbency. The cotton balls work great with pee, but if you get poop you may need something a bit larger to do the clean up. I like using regular infant baby wipes, but always use ones with no alcohol, perfume, or dye. Just keep stroking until the little guy is done, and don't be surprised if it takes awhile.

Group two (11 days to 2-1/2 weeks) kittens will be starting to exercise some control of their bodily functions. This means that sometimes, especially if there are several littermates, you will go to feed them and find them covered with "stuff." Remember that you should be proud that they were able to do it by themselves! You can start skipping the stimulating every couple of feedings to give them an opportunity to go on their own.

Group three (2-1/2 weeks to 4 weeks) kitten are ready to start controlling this process. Stimulate the younger ones a couple of times a day with feedings, but by the end of this age group they should not need your assistance.

Group four (4 weeks and older) kittens do not need stimulating.

Cleaning and bathing

Group one (0 to 10 days) kittens can be bathed, but great care must be taken to be very gentle and to protect them from getting chilled. Unless absolutely necessary, don't bathe them until after the umbilical cord has fallen off. The bathroom sink or a shallow basin inside the kitchen sink are easy places. Water that is comfortably warm to your wrists is fine. You can use kitten shampoo if you like, providing it is free from chemicals. Do NOT use products with pesticides, such as anti-flea stuff, as long as it is a "no tears" formula. Plain old baby shampoo works just fine, as long as it is thoroughly rinsed from the skin. I always let the shampoo bottle sit in hot water first, so that it won't chill the baby.

When you are ready, carefully hold the baby with it's head supported above the water, then lift it up and put the shampoo on top of the head and down the back. Gently work it in with your fingers all over the body, and then continue the same stroking motions with the baby back in the water for rinsing. The final rinsing can be under running warm water from the tap, but be careful to avoid getting water in the nose or ears. By the way, don't be surprised if your washing motions act like stimulation. It only means that the baby had to go. If it grosses you out to get a "handful," just remember that it all washes off and isn't harmful. Don't panic during the bath just because the water has stuff in it. Knowing this might happen in advance, though, might affect your choice of where you want to do the bathing -- lots of people prefer cleaning the bathroom sink of "stuff" rather than the kitchen.

The most important part is thorough drying. After toweling the kitten off, a handheld hair dryer works just fine, as long as you make sure it is not too hot. A good rule of thumb is your own comfort. If the hot air is too hot for your hand, it is too hot for the kitten and needs to be turned down. After the bath be sure to put the baby in a well-warmed bed, with a heat source, away from any drafts.

In between baths you can keep the kittens reasonably clean using baby-wipes. Any brand will do, as long as it is free of alcohol, perfumes or dyes. These are awfully handy to keep by the carriers anyway, for those times when your fingers desperately need cleaning.

Group two (11 days to 2-1/2 weeks) kittens get absolutely disgusting at times, so bathing is very important. Since these kittens are beginning to develop some body function control, they react quickly to stimulation from anything that rubs their body. This means that when you go to feed the little darlings they are frequently soaking wet and covered with poop. First of all, remember that you can't possibly keep them clean as their mother could. Just use the baby-wipes each time you pick them up as needed, and bathe them when the wipes just can't do the job. The procedure is the same as for Group one kittens, outlined above.

Group three (2-1.2 weeks to 4 weeks) kittens are startling to learn how to use their litterboxes, and sometimes even attempt to groom themselves or their littermates. They are a little cleaner than Group two, but the bathing procedures are the same.

Group four (4 weeks and older) kittens should be doing a pretty good job of using the litterbox and basic grooming. Unless they are longhaired, with litter and food and waste stuck in their fur, bathing should rarely be needed. If you need to bathe them, the same steps as for the other groups do just fine.

Litterbox Training

Group three (2-1/2 weeks to 4 weeks) kittens will start looking for an absorbent place to go to the bathroom. The age will vary with the individuals, but the time to start putting a litterbox into the cage is as soon as the kitten walks fully upright, even though they might still be wobbly. Just watch for them to graduate from the "low crawl" to getting the bellies off the ground and put in a very shallow litter box. Disposable aluminum cookie sheets or baking pans work very well, and are cheap. They will still be messing in their bedding and throughout the cage while learning, but the presence of the box will eventually let their instincts teach them.

You can assist the process by observing the locations they start to use, then put the litter box in that spot -- even though where you wanted to put it may be much more logical to you. If they like the spot, putting the box there helps them make the proper connection. Do NOT scratch their paws in the litter to try to teach them to use the box or cover what they did. All you do is scare them, and that sets the process back.

Group four (4 weeks and older) kittens should be doing a pretty good job of using the litterbox, but they will still make mistakes. They also are like little kids and will play until they just can't wait. When that happens they will look for the closest appropriate place to go. To protect your corners, rugs, papers, etc., do not let them play for extended periods in too large an area away from their boxes. And don't get too stressed with the mistakes. Just clean it up and realize that they will master the litterbox as they get older.

Weaning

Group four (4 weeks and older) kittens are ready for the weaning process. Again, this is an individual thing, as some kittens will explore food at a slightly younger age; however, like children, this process should not be rushed as doing so can cause digestive problems. Remember also that kittens normally learn to eat food my mimicking their mother. Letting the kittens play around your adult cats when they are eating is a great teaching aid for the weaning process.

Just a note about the special weaning foods available that are produced by the companies that make the kitten formula. Please save your money! While these may be nutritiously perfect, I have never seen a kitten that would willingly eat it, and have seen adult cats try to bury it. The point is very simple, if the food does not have smell and taste appeal, the kittens will not be interested in trying it.

Weaning should be a gradual process, generally starting about 4 weeks of age. Use very shallow dishes that cannot be tipped over. Start by adding about 2 parts water to 1 part dry kitten food in your microwave for about a minute or so. Then let the mixture sit so that the water can all be absorbed. Some brands take longer than others, but the result is soft, like canned food. It is not a good idea to use formula for the mixture, since formula can go rancid when allowed to sit, and you are trying to entice the kittens into a different food source. Mix about equal parts softened dry food with canned food for smell and taste appeal. Some kittens will discover the stuff by themselves, while others need your assistance. If they need help figuring out what the food is for, you can try gently putting their mouth in the food so they can lick it off. Don't force or rub their faces into the mix, since that would just scare them. A very good method is to try using a plastic spoon and putting a small amount in their mouth so they can see what it tastes like. If they like it, just keep using the spoon and lowering it down so they can see that the dish has the food. This process will definitely take patience, and a sense of humor. At first they will suck at the food and dish, sort of expecting this new food to jump in like the bottle formula. They will also get absolutely filthy. They will walk in the food, sit in the food dish, track food all over the cage and into the litterbox, then walk back through the food with the litter stuck all over them. Don't panic and don't worry about bathing after every meal. A cleaning with a babywipe will do fine until the next time.

Fresh weaning food should be put into the cage about as often as you are providing bottles, which at this point would be about four times a day. Remember that bottles should only be given after the fresh food has been offered, so they don't fill up first on formula. Leave the food for them until you replace it at the next feeding, because is is important for the kittens to have it available for exploration. Replacing it each time, even if very little was eaten, is equally important because the food will get so dirty. As the kittens eat more and more, gradually cut back on the number of bottles offered. Generally the kittens will let you know when they are no longer interested in the bottles. I do not recommend just taking the bottle away when you think they are doing well enough on solid food, because the bottle also represents comfort and nurturing. Taking a kitten off the bottle before it is ready can result in problems later in life, such as sucking on an owner's arm or hand or sucking and kneading on blankets or clothing. Any behaviors that might be viewed as odd or negative can result in a cat losing its home, so taking care in advance to avoid creation of those habits is very important.

Playing

Playing is just as important and educational for kittens as it is for children. For this reason, kittens need adequate room to play as they grow up, as well as age appropriate safe toys. Remember that play and sleep are both important and must be balanced.

Play is an activity in which kittens learn from each other. This means that if a kitten is raised alone he will miss out on some very important lessons that you cannot teach him. Only another kitten can teach him that teeth and claws hurt, which is why kittens raised alone are frequently much too rough in their play as teenagers and adults. Play is also an area where adult cats can be excellent mentors and companions. Only an adult cat can teach an overly rambunctious kitten proper cat etiquette and manners, so do not keep your adults and kittens separated just because you are afraid the adults will be too rough. They may indeed be a little rough, but with very rare exceptions they will be teaching the babies, not hurting them. So if your adult cat is playing with a kitten and the kitten starts howling, don't immediately jump in to rescue the baby or punish the adult cat. Chances are that the baby is just being restrained and doesn't like it. Kittens need to learn respect for adults and this is the only way that lesson can be taught. If you interfere, the chances for a successful adoption of your kittens into households with resident adults can be severely reduced.

Nail Trimming

Needle sharp nails can get in an eye or tender nose, as well as human skin, so keeping the nails trimmed is very important. In addition, when a kitten has had its feet and nails handled from babyhood, it is less likely to "shred" an owner as an adult. Trimming a cat or kitten's nails is much easier than trying to do a dog's nails. As long as you just cut off the hook portion of the nail, you don't have to worry about hurting the baby or cutting into the nail quick and causing bleeding. You can purchase special trimmers for cats, which work very well. I prefer plain old human nail clippers.

Nail trimming should be quickly and easily done, and should never be a fight. Remember that cats hate to be restrained, so hold them loosely on your lap and then gently press on the top of each toe of the foot to make the nail extend. Quickly snip off the hook, then move on to the next one. Most people just clip the front claws, since they are the ones used in play or for sharpening. Taking your time and giving the kitten lots of petting and soft talk so the process is pleasant will make a huge difference.

Weighing

Tracking the weight of a kitten is one of the absolutely best ways to be sure they are growing properly, and to catch problems before they become disasters. Daily weighing and charting of kittens is as important as anything else you can do for them. Be sure to weigh consistently, by that I mean at about the same time each day. Also, be sure to be consistent in weighing in relationship to feeding. For example, if you weigh one day after has gorged on breakfast, then weigh the next day when they first wake up, you'll think something awful is happening to cause major weight loss. There is no right time or system, just be consistent so the weight gain or loss is not just a meal.

A good rule of thumb is to expect about 1/2 ounce gain per day, slightly more with older kittens. If you see no gain or even a loss over three days, something is probably going wrong. Do an evaluation of behavior patterns to see what changes might be happening, then contact your mentor for suggestions on what to do next. Don't wait until the kittens are visibly failing before taking action!

Chapter 4

Potential problems and how to handle them

Any foster home, no matter how clean, careful, observant, or downright paranoid they may be, will deal with all or most of these conditions eventually. The advice given here is anecdotal, and not designed to replace or refute what you might hear from your vet. Before you throw out anecdotal advise, however, remember that it came from dealing with hundreds of kittens, most likely many more orphan kittens than your vet has personally dealt with. So be observant, stay in touch with your experienced mentor, and try these suggestions before you run to the vet's office.

No Weight Gain

This is always a clue to a problem, but pinpointing the problem can be a real puzzle. Never ignore a failure to grow -- and that means 3 consecutive days of loss or no gain. A thorough evaluation needs to take place first, so check to see if there are any signs of illness such as weepy or goopy eyes, runny nose, sneezing, constipation or diarrhea. If so, treat the symptoms. Next, check the temperature. Normal temperature for kittens is 101 - 102. Low or elevated temperature could provide clues to an underlying problem, which then needs to be addressed. If you are still striking out for clues, make sure that you are providing enough nourishment. That means not only feeding often enough, but with a food that they are really enjoying. If the food you are providing is not being eaten, change it and see it that solves the problem within a day or two. Please note that this "changing food" advise does NOT apply to kittens that are still on the bottle!

If you cannot identify the reason for this problem, start the kitten on a broad spectrum antibiotic, such as clavamox. If the antibiotic doesn't help the kitten gaining weight within about 3 days, then you will need to have it checked out by your mentor or vet.

Constipation

Constipation generally falls into two different categories, kittens that continuously have hard stools or kittens with a temporary problem causing a hard, dry "plug" blocking the anus.

Constant constipation is almost always diet related, which means that until they are weaned this type is very rare. The easiest, gentlest solution for kittens that are still on the bottle is to mix the formula with whole cows milk (whole milk, not reduced fat or nonfat,) starting with a half-and-half mixture. This will usually take a day or so to make a difference. If nothing changes, the ratio of milk can be increased. Once the stools are normal you can gradually decrease the amount of milk. Some rare kittens will need a mixture until they are weaned. Constipated kittens that are either completely weaned or in the weaning process should have their solid kitten food changed until you find a kind that does not create the problem.

The more common, temporary constipation problem is best overcome by manual methods, starting with the simplest and least invasive. Mineral oil massaged gently all over the anus with a q-tip after feeding will often provide enough stimulation and lubrication to solve the problem. Mineral oil should NOT be put into the food in an attempt to lubricate internally. If this does not do the trick after a day, you can use a well-lubricated thermometer (digital or oral, since you need a narrow tip). Use mineral oil or petroleum jelly as a lubricant, and then gently insert the thermometer. Very gently and very slowly move the thermometer in and out, and twist it round and round. You need to be very gentle, since you are just trying to lubricate and carefully open up the sphincter muscle. If a plug is blocking the entrance you should see fecal material on the thermometer when it is slowly withdrawn. Doing this a couple of times during a 24 hour period will almost always help the kitten go. If it does not, the last resort is an enema, but you should have someone experienced help you to avoid hurting the kitten.

Diarrhea

This is one of the most common and most serious problems that occur with orphan babies. It is also a problem that can be caused by a variety of causes. The four general causes are stress, diet, medication, and parasites. The treatment will depend on the cause and the age of the kittens.

Stress can be caused by a multitude of things. Changes in the environment can be a major cause, particularly in older kittens since they are more aware of their surroundings. Avoid stress by keeping the kittens' environment as calm, stable, safe and comfortable as possible. When a sudden case of diarrhea happens, always check for the quality of the kittens' area, and for any recent changes that might have taken place in the immediate surroundings or in the household.

Diet is a huge cause of diarrhea, and can usually be cured quickly. Unweaned kittens will frequently get diarrhea if you change the formula, even as simple a change as keeping the brand but going from liquid to powder formula. As long as the food quality is the same, diarrhea caused by a formula change should quickly resolve itself. Food quality is a huge issue with kittens that are starting on solid foods. Poor quality foods (grocery and generic store brands, and the super cheap brands) will very often cause diarrhea. And just because a food is labeled "kitten", does not mean it is good quality. There are some very good quality brands made for all ages. You need to check with your mentor or vet to make sure the brand you are using is providing the nutrition the kittens need. In some rare cases a particular high quality brand is just too rich for an individual kitten, so trying a different brand may solve the problem.

Medication, particularly antibiotics, can often cause diarrhea. It is not only a side effect of the medicine, but also because the medication strips the intestinal tract of beneficial bacterial. For this reason it is a good idea to replenish the healthy bacteria through the use of probiotics whenever you use medication, an always when diarrhea starts shortly after you begin medicating. There are several good brands of probiotics available, so check with your mentor or vet for a recommendation.

The last cause of diarrhea can be parasites, such as worms, coccydia or giardia. These conditions can generally be diagnosed by a fecal test, although experienced foster moms can often know just by the odor or appearance of the diarrhea when some of the parasites are present. Experienced foster mentors, especially those working within rescue groups, can often provide medication for the parasites.

Regardless of the cause, diarrhea must not be ignored because it can be lethal if not treated promptly.

Dehydration

Dehydration is deadly and cannot be ignored. To test for dehydration, use your thumb and forefinger to gently lift the skin between the shoulder blades. If the skin drops right down, the kitten is not dehydrated. If the skin stays tented up the kitten needs to be hydrated by subcutaneous fluids. This condition cannot be cured through fluids by mouth, so be sure to contact your vet or foster mentor right away. This condition is urgent, so "right away" means within hours, NOT days! Learning to hydrate is a very important skill if you are going to continue to foster.

Loss of appetite

Loss of appetite is something that cannot be ignored, and can be caused by a variety of different things.

Group one (0 to 10 days) Loss of appetite in this age group can be a very serious, even deadly, symptom. When the kitten shows no interest in a feeding make sure it is clean and warm, and watch it very closely the next time. If it is not interested the next feeding time, start treatment for hypoglycemic shock, or low blood sugar, just in case. See the section on hypoglycemic shock for directions on how to proceed. If low blood sugar is the problem, you should see an increase in the appetite the next feeding. Please not that the karo syrup should be administered slowly, drop by drop, from the syringe so the baby can swallow it or absorb the sugar in it's mouth without worrying about choking or aspirating. If the kitten continues to show no interest in feeding, especially if the muscle tone feels flaccid, the kitten may die. As a last resort you might also try subcutaneous fluids to help keep their fluid level up and start it on an antibiotic such as clavamox. Kittens this young have very little reserves to tide them over being sick, but this regimen will sometimes bring them back if started early.

If the kitten does not improve, please don't beat yourself up emotionally over the death. No one knows why this happens -- vets call it either "failure to thrive," or "failing kitten syndrome" -- which just means that they don't know the reason for the death. Watching a kitten die is an extraordinarily difficult thing to do, but unfortunately it will happen to everyone who fosters babies, especially those brave souls who specialize in taking the very young ones. My rule of thumb has always been to keep the baby warm and comfortable and just let it slip deep into coma and pass on its own, providing it is not in pain. If it is fighting and in pain it is more merciful to take it in and have it put down, but generally that is not necessary.

Group two (11 days to 2-1/2 weeks) Loss of appetite in this group is handled just like Group one, except that you need to evaluate the frequency of the feedings in addition to the other possibilities. That is particularly true if more than one of the kittens seems less interested in eating. You can test that theory by moving the second back an extra 30 minutes to see if they do better.

Group three (1 days to 2-1/2 weeks) Loss of appetite in this group is usually a sign that some problem is just starting to develop, but can also be related to the start of the weaning process for ones at the older end of the spectrum. Babies that are only on the bottle can lose interest if the feeding frequency is too close, it can be a sign of low blood sugar (see group one directions above), or even a very early sign of some type of virus or bacterial infection. Follow the steps outlined above for kittens that are completely on the bottle. Kittens in this age group will sometimes show little interest in a bottle because they are discovering the joys of solid food and full tummies. Never count on that answer, however, unless you are positive that they are eating solid foods.

Group four (4 weeks and older) Kittens in this group should be in the weaning process, so you must watch their weight gain and other clues instead of just depending on their interest in the bottle at a feeding. In, in addition to not looking hungry, the kitten appears to be listless or glassy-eyed, check for low blood sugar and run through the karo syrup regimen (every 20 minutes for up to 2 hours). If that is the cause, you should see a marked change within the karo syrup treatment time.

Temperature change

A normal kitten temperature will range from 101 to 102. Temperatures should be checked routinely when you think that something is not normal with behavior, eating patterns or weight gain. Remember that a below normal temperature is just as dangerous as a high temperature and must not be ignored.

If a kitten has a below normal temperature but is still alert, the first step is to try to warm it up externally. Wrap the kitten in heated towels or baby blankets and place it in a small carrier or cage with a heat source (rice pack, etc.). Check the temperature in about a half hour for progress. If this method brings the temperature to normal then you can be reasonably sure that the temperature was just from outside environment, but watch the kitten carefully for the next couple of days. If there is very little or no change, treat the kitten with karo syrup for low blood sugar (hypoglycemic shock). If that does the trick you know you caught it early. Generally there are no long-term ill effects, but you should still watch closely for any repeated bouts of low blood sugar.

If your kitten's temperature is very low (I've seen 94) it is probably virtually comatose. IF this is a kitten that has been behaving normally in your care that has collapsed suddenly, the cause is generally low blood sugar (hypoglycemic shock). In addition to the karo syrup and heated towels, you need to administer warmed subcutaneous fluids to "jump-start" the temperature internally. If you can't do the fluids yourself, contact your mentor or vet immediately, because this is not a situation that can wait.

High temperatures in a kitten are generally due to either a serious infection or possibly to a vaccine reaction. If the temperature is moderately high (103 to 104), starting a regimen of broad-spectrum antibiotics (like clavamox) will generally bring it down pretty quickly. If it is very high (105 or more), you need to get it down immediately in addition to treating the underlying cause. Use a wet towel on the ears, face and paws, since this will help the body temperature without too much stress on the animal or risking shock by getting the whole body wet. You should also administer room temperature subcutaneous fluids to cool the fluids internally. If you can't do the fluids yourself, contact your mentor or vet for help. If the temperature is extremely high (106 or higher) cool the body by wetting the ears, face and paws, then get it to a vet immediately.

Sudden collapse

The key to this condition is whether or not it is really "sudden." A sudden collapse of an otherwise healthy, active kitten is almost always best handled as a low blood sugar (hypoglycemic shock) episode, with karo syrup. A collapse can also occur when there is illness or weight loss that has not been observed. If that is the case, appropriate immediate supportive care is required to get over the episode, then treatment for the underlying problem. If the kitten that collapsed was not healthy, active and of a normal weight, it needs to be seen by a mentor or vet to determine the probable cause and best treatment.

Lethargy

This condition is often the precursor of a "sudden collapse," so the treatment is handled very similarly. The key, just like the "sudden collapse," is whether or not it is truly sudden or not. Lethargy in a normally healthy, active kitten can be the start or either a low blood sugar (hypoglycemic shock) episode, or the start of a bacterial or viral infection of some kind. If the temperature is subnormal, treat it like low blood sugar with karo syrup. If that solves the problem, just watch for future episodes. If it does not make a difference or if the temperature is normal, treat with a broad-spectrum antibiotic (like clavamox) just in case. As always, you need to work closely with your mentor and/or vet.

Lethargy in a kitten that was not healthy, active and of a normal weight indicates that the underlying problem is getting more serious. This kitten needs to be seen by a mentor or vet to determine the probable cause and best treatment.

If you take a lethargic kitten into your home, check the temperature, weight, dehydration and mouth. If the temperature, weight, or dehydration levels are not good, handle accordingly. If the mouth and gums are gray or white instead of healthy pink, the kitten probably has flea anemia and needs to be treated accordingly.

Fleas / Flea anemia

Fleas should never be a problem in a foster home. All animals should be regularly treated with Advantage, Frontline, or other safe products, to protect them. Be extremely careful using other flea treatment products from your local pet store, drug store, discount store or grocery store. Be particularly careful purchasing or using products that say "like Advantage" or "like Frontline" and are half the price. Many of those products are toxic or even lethal to cats.

When kittens arrive covered with fleas, and many will, it is imperative that they be bathed and treated with an acceptable topical flea treatment (like Advantage or Frontline). The bath and flea treatment need to be 24 hours apart, so the decision on which to do first will depend on the condition of the animal and number of fleas. If the infestation is really bad, there are topical treatments (like Capstan) that will kill all the fleas immediately, but have no residual effect. That can be used before the bath to help provide immediate relief, with the long term flea treatment (like Advantage or Frontline) to be administered 24 hours after the bath.

A kitten that arrives infested with fleas needs to have its mouth and gums carefully checked. The color of the mouth and gums should be a healthy pink. If it is gray or white, the kitten is suffering from flea anemia, which means that the blood has literally been sucked out of it. This condition is life threatening. A severely anemic kitten may die before the body can rebuild the blood supply. The only course of actual treatment for severe flea anemia is a blood transfusion, but that is a very expensive proposition. In most cases it is just not a reasonable option for a young, very ill, orphan kitten in foster care. Providing supportive care while the baby's body rebuilds is usually all you can do, and in all but the worst cases it generally works. The kitten will be weak and lethargic for days or weeks while it recovers and needs to be closely monitored.

Kittens that arrive infested with fleas are also prime candidates for tapeworm infestations. Tapeworm larvae are carried by the fleas, so will appear a couple of weeks after you think the flea problem has been solved. Watch for the symptoms and see your mentor or vet for the proper worming medication. Be very careful using over the counter tapeworm treatments for young kittens, and never without approval of your mentor or vet.

Hypoglycemic shock (low blood sugar)

Hypoglycemic shock, which just means low blood sugar levels, can kill. It is also one of the easiest conditions to treat and one of the fastest to respond to treatment. You cannot predict in advance which kittens will develop this, nor which kittens might have repeat episodes. Vets do not even know for sure what causes it, although they believe that immature livers may be the underlying cause. If you run to the vet with a kitten with low blood sugar, they will treat with dextrose (sugar), so your treatment is with old-fashioned karo syrup (white corn syrup for cooking). Every kitten foster parent should always keep karo syrup on hand. It is cheap and easily available at any grocery store, but when you need it you cannot wait or waste time.

Using a simple syringe administer about .15 (that is POINT 15 of a mil) in the mouth about every 20 to 30 minutes until the kitten is back on its feet with a normal temperature and behavior. If the kitten has collapsed and/or has a severely depressed temperature, contact your mentor or vet immediately because the kitten will need subcutaneous fluids in addition to the karo syrup. If the kitten is comatose when you start, just gently put it in the mouth so that the membranes will absorb some of the sugar. Don't try to make a comatose kitten swallow or you could cause the baby to aspirate the karo syrup into the lungs or choke. If, after about 2 hours of regular doses, you have seen no change, get the kitten to your mentor or vet for evaluation and additional treatment.

Worms

Worms are probably the most common parasites you will encounter with kittens. The two most common kinds are round worms and tape worms. Round worms are very damaging to the kittens system, while the medicine seldom causes difficulty. For this reason I recommend routinely treating for round worms in all kittens. Starting at about 10 days old you give a round worm treatment (such as strongid), then do it again in 10 days. It is very important that you do the treatments 10 days apart because the medicine only kills the actual worms in the intestinal tract. The second worming kills the newly hatched worms before they can mature and lay new eggs. Tapeworms are relatively easy on the kitten's body, while the medicine is very strong. For this reason you may be advised to only treat for tapeworms when you have seen signs of them. If you kitten has small white bits that look like grains of rice near it's rectum, it has tapeworms. Of course, if you see worms in the kittens' stool, treat immediately. Round worms are long, light brown and round like earthworms. Tapeworms are white, flat and segmented. If you suspect worms but don't know what you are seeing, contact your mentor or get a fecal test done by your vet. Do NOT use an over-the-counter worm medicine from the pet store or grocery store on young kittens!

Upper respiratory infections

This is probably the most common illness in young kittens, and deadly if not treated. Symptoms include sneezing, runny eyes, runny noses, fever, lethargy, etc. You must start them on a broad-spectrum antibiotic (like clavamox) immediately, plus try to relive the discomfort of the symptoms themselves. Make sure the kittens are warm, dry and free of drafts. Gently clean the noses and eyes to prevent crusting and additional infection. If the eyes are discharging green or yellow mucus, see your mentor or vet for eye medication, and use it religiously as instructed. If breathing is difficult through a stuffy nose, you can put the carrier in the bathroom and fill the room with steam, just like you would do for a child, then make sure the kittens are dry before leaving the warm room. You may need to change the food while they are ill to encourage them to eat, because nothing tastes when you can't smell it. Watch the weight closely and stay in touch with your mentor or vet. You must stay very observant to any changes to get them through safely.

Failure to thrive

In years past this is what vets used to give as the reason why young kittens would die. In spite of your very best efforts sometimes kittens will die for no apparent reason, especially those that are orphaned with their umbilical cords still attached. We know more now, and you can benefit from all the hard lessons learned by other foster people throughout the years. Your constant diligence and close monitoring of these babies give them a much better chance of survival, so that someday, this term might not be used anymore.

"A.D.R.", (Ain"t Doing Right)

This is the very official sounding diagnosis vets give, or put on cage cards in their clinics, when they know something is wrong but just don't know what it is. If this is the best description you can come up with to give your mentor or vet, trust your own judgment! You know your kitten better than anyone, and you know when it "ain't doing right." Before you call your mentor or vet for help, go through your checklist:

- Is it eating, drinking and going potty?
- Have the eating, drinking or potty habits changed?
- How has the weight gain pattern been?
- What is the temperature?
- Is the kitten alert and active?
- Are there any symptoms of illness?

If you come up with any answers from the checklist, try the suggestions outlined in these pages and monitor the results. If you find no answers or if your attempts to help have not worked, don't doubt yourself. Call the mentor or vet and go through everything with them. You will save time and gain credibility if you call with all the basics covered in advance.

Chapter 5

Routine Treatments

Your goal as a kitten parent is to raise healthy, happy kittens for great families. In addition to the routine growth stages we have outlined, there are routine treatments that are an important part of the process.

Deworming

Because worms are the most common parasites, I recommend routinely treating for round worms in all kittens. Starting at about 10 days old you give a round worm treatment (such as strongid), then do it again in 10 days. It is very important that you do the treatments 10 days apart because the medicine only kills the actual worms in the intestinal tract. The second worming kills the newly hatched worms before they can mature and lay new eggs. Tapeworms are relatively easy on the kitten's body, while the medicine is very strong. For this reason you may be advised to only treat for tapeworms when you have seen signs of them. If you kitten has small white bits that look like grains of rice near it's rectum, it has tapeworms. Of course, if you see worms in the kittens' stool, treat immediately. Round worms are long, light brown and round like earthworms. Tapeworms are white, flat and segmented. If you suspect worms but don't know what you are seeing, contact your mentor or get a fecal test done by your vet. Do NOT use an over-the-counter worm medicine from the pet store or grocery store on young kittens!

Leukemia testing

Leukemia testing is very important before you place a kitten for adoption. Tests can be done on saliva or with blood. Contact your mentor or vet to make the arrangements. You seldom need to test all the kittens in a litter, generally you will just test one kitten or do a batch test combining blood of two or more from the litter. If you get a positive result, you will need to wait and then retest to rule out false positives.

Kitten vaccinations

There a variety of brands and types of kitten vaccines available. The type and brand is not as important as having the vaccines given at the appropriate times, and also the proper dosage. For many years we, many rescue people and myself, have been using a 1/2 dose of vaccine for kittens 3 pounds and under. A normal vaccine is for cats and kittens 5 to 15 pounds, so the reduced dose still provides the same amount of immunity, with less chance for a vaccine reaction. In fact, after about 10 years of using 1/2 a vaccine for small kittens, we have not seen a single vaccine reaction. Vaccine reactions, especially in small kittens, can be very severe and even fatal, so this is a significant safety issue.

Vaccines should only be given to healthy, thriving babies, never to ones that are ill or significantly underweight. First vaccines are normally given at 9 weeks; however, for orphan kittens I recommend giving the first vaccine at 6 weeks, with the 2nd. and 3rd. at 3-week intervals. Starting at a younger age won't hurt the babies, but does not provide some protection at an earlier age. This is extremely important if you have numerous foster animals coming into the home. Many vaccines recommend the last dose (the one lasts for the first year) be given at about 15 weeks. If the 3rd. vaccine is given to a much younger kitten, you may need to give a 4th. vaccine for full protection.

Most kittens handle their vaccines with no problems at all, but if one of them does get sick after receiving an injection, contact your mentor or vet immediately.

Topical flea treatment (Advantage or Frontline)

Kittens must be kept free of fleas because of the danger of flea anemia and tapeworms, not to mention the sheer misery of the pests. Do NOT use flea collars, powders, pet store or grocery store flea treatments for kittens. Both Advantage and Frontline are relatively inexpensive and very safe. You can use either brand for very young kittens as long as you use the proper dose. Empty the tube into a small container (baby food jar, medicine bottle, etc.) with a good tight lid, then syringe out just what you need. An easy rule of thumb is one drop per pound for the kittens. One drop is safe for the tiniest baby, administered between the shoulder blades on the skin.

Do it every 30 days and you will not have to worry about fleas and the diseases they carry.

With the original Advantage or Frontline formulations we were able to save a lot of money by purchasing the big dog version and using the proper dosage for cats and kittens. That is still a great savings for the basic formulations of these brands, but you must check with your mentor or vet first. You cannot use versions that contain heartworm medication, since the dosage will not be right or safe for kittens. It is extremely important that you NOT use flea treatment brands that advertise "as good as Advantage or Frontline", since many of them are toxic or even lethal for cats and kittens. Read labels carefully and check with your mentor or vet before trying anything other than regular Advantage or Frontline for kittens.

Spaying & neutering

As a foster parent you play a vital part in helping overcome the pet overpopulation problem. For this reason you need to make sure that no animal leaving your care can ever reproduce. An experienced vet easily does early spaying and neutering, but be sure to use a vet or clinic that offers reduced rates for rescue.

Many vets and organizations will do kittens as early as 6 weeks and as small as 1 pound. Most kittens come through the surgery, even though there is a significant statistical survival rate difference. The thinking behind this is simple -- "if they die under anesthesia it is unfortunate, but there are hundreds more out there and people want to adopt little tiny kittens." A better plan, and one based on the animal's needs rather than the somewhat unrealistic and thoughtless desires of the adopting public, is to wait until the animal is healthy and weighs 3 pounds. This insures a much better outcome, with a lower possibility of complications during or after surgery.

First they start out like this, all tiny and adorable.....

.....and then they get even cuter and more precious!

This baby stayed with us. Here she is all grown up

Chapter 6

Placing your kittens in new homes

Your job as foster parent is to raise healthy, well adjusted kittens for great homes. Parting with them is very hard, but placing them with families that will love them and care for them throughout their lives is enormously satisfying. It also means that you will be available for the next little ones who need you so badly. Adoptions are the final responsibility of the foster parent, so here are some suggestions.

If you are a member of a rescue group they will undoubtedly have requirements and standards for all prospective homes. All the rules are there for a reason and you are morally obligated to follow their guidelines for placement. If you don't like the rules, consider working with another group in the future. If you are fostering outside of a group it is up to you to make the decisions. Your careful consideration and thorough screening of prospective homes is vital for the health and safety of the baby you worked so hard to save. You need to make your own decisions, but here are some of my adoptive guidelines.

Placement age

Some groups will place kittens as young as 6 to 8 weeks old, but I recommend waiting until they are about 12 weeks old. The additional time permits them to reach the weight limit to get spayed or neutered and for you to complete the series of 3 vaccines. This extra time also insures a healthier, more confident kitten that is less likely to get stressed out and sick from the move. Kittens this age are also much less likely to make litter box mistakes in their new homes or have other behavior problems when removed from their littermates.

Adoption fee

If you are working within a group, the adoption fee will be set in advance. If you are fostering independently, you need to determine a reasonable amount to charge to help cover the expenses for raising the kittens, as well as what local groups in your area are charging. You will never make money on fostering, but it is very important that you not get so eager to place your kittens that you let them go without charging a fee. Whatever you do, NEVER place on a "free to good home" basis!

There are four very compelling reasons not to adopt out "free" kittens:

#1   People often place a value on things based on what they cost. You do not want people that view the babies as disposable just because they were free.

#2   People wanting free kittens often cannot afford a pet. Just because they can buy bags of food and litter on sale at the grocery store does not mean they can afford to meet all your kitten's needs. You need owners that will provide quality nutrition and proper vet care when necessary. Kittens are a lifetime commitment and they are expensive, so be sure that the new family is prepared meet that commitment for the next 15 to 20 years.

#3   People who want free kittens and puppies are sometimes looking for animals they can acquire and resell to laboratories for experimentation. Your adoption fee removes the profit motive and saves your precious baby from life as a lab animal.

#4   People who want free kittens and puppies are sometimes looking for animals to use as bait to train fighting dogs. If you are not vigilant and protective, the baby you raised so carefully may face a horrible death.
Don't be fooled by people wanting free animals, no matter how nice and sincere they may seem. If you are taken in by a well crafted story, your babies will pay the price.

Inside cats only

My single most important requirement is that the kitten will be kept inside 100% of the time for 100% of its life. No exceptions for large properties, back porches, fenced yards, etc. This means no adoptions to homes with doggy doors to the outside, because the kitten will definitely learn to use it. It also means no adoptions to a household with inside-outside cats, because when the kitten and the resident cats bond, the kitten will want to follow its friend outside and eventually the family will let it happy. The reason for this is very simple -- cats that are inside-only live a statistical average of 7 times longer than cats allowed outside. Most rescue groups and shelters have this requirement now for the safety of the animals they adopt out. It is even more crucial for bottle-fed orphans, because these babies have never been taught to fear anything and are incredibly vulnerable.

Renters

The people who adopt your kittens need to either own their own homes or have written landlord permission. If they are renters, make sure they have made arrangements with the landlord or property management company to have the kitten. You might feel uncomfortable asking these questions and requiring written proof, but it will be much worse if the people who take your kitten come back to you in a couple of weeks or months, tears in their eyes, to return the kitten because they are not allowed to have it. And imagine how you would feel if you found out someone who adopted the baby you raised so lovingly took it to the shelter when they got caught and were too embarrassed to contact you when they were threatened with eviction!

Declawing

All cats need to sharpen their claws, but there are ways to provide them acceptable locations and alternatives to clawing furniture or carpets. Scratching posts are available in all sizes and types, so experiment until you find what your kitten likes, and be sure to share that information with the adoptive family. Keeping the kittens' nails trimmed short is a great help, and demonstrating the technique and its importance to the adoptive family should be part of the adoption process. You can also recommend soft claw covers called "Soft Paws" if the family has concerns about clawing. I would not adopt to a family that was planning to declaw their kitten. This should only be done as an absolute last resort. This is one subject that definitely must be covered in depth and in advance of any adoption.

Families with young children

Many groups have absolute guidelines about adopting to homes with young children. Some refuse to place kittens in families with children below a certain age. Rather than use an arbitrary age, I like to see the children and kittens together. I am most concerned with the way the children behave with the animals and the way the parents monitor and correct their kids. While some young children are very patient and good with kittens, it is still never a good idea to put small kittens with small children. Families with kids 3 or younger should adopt "teen-age" (6 months to a year old) kittens or young adult cats. This way you don't have to worry about protecting the babies from accidentally hurting each other.

Screening applicants for adoption

Careful screening is critical for successful adoptions. If you run ads in local papers or online services, be sure to screen very carefully on the phone first. If you don't get the right answers on the phone or if someone sounds a bit odd, just thank them and get off the phone. If you aren't comfortable talking to someone on the phone, you don't want them to have your kittens -- and you definitely do not want them coming to your home.

Remember that you are in control of the adoption process, and trust your instincts. You have invested an enormous amount of energy, love, time and money to raise your babies, so take the time to find the right homes. It's a good idea to have a written contract that clearly and concisely spells out your adoption requirements, terms and fees. Rescue groups will have adoption agreements already prepared in advance, or you can prepare one yourself. The agreement needs to have the personal information for the foster parent and adoptive family, as well as all the terms everyone has agreed to. Any agreement needs to include very clear language regarding what is supposed to happen if the adoption does not work out, or if the kitten needs to be surrendered to the foster family for cause. The agreement should also have all the pertinent statistics and medical information for the kitten. Remember that both parties should have a signed copy of the agreement before the kitten is taken to its new home.

Made in the USA
Middletown, DE
24 June 2015